Beach Blanket Bistro

Tropically Inspired Cuisine

Recipes by Shannon Stiles

Photos by Christa Stiles

Disclaimer

Consuming raw or undercooked food may increase your risk of food borne illness. People most at risk are children, the elderly, and persons with a weakened immune system.

Neither the publisher nor the author takes any responsibility for any possible consequences of any person reading or following the information and instructions in this book.

For more information:

www.beachblanketbistro.com

ISBN: 978-0-692-96925-0

Acknowledgements

This project started simple. I had no idea what I was getting myself into or how exactly I was going to do it. There are so many people to thank that I can't possibly list them all, so I am only going to mention a few key players that assisted me in putting this together.

First of all, I have to thank my wife, Christa. She has supported my many endeavors over the past twenty plus years. She is also the photographer and designer for the entire project. I would also like to thank my dear friend, Eleanor, who has kept me motivated and has been indispensable in the promotion of Beach Blanket Bistro. Lastly, I'd like to thank Steve. He expressed enough belief in my talent that I felt I could actually pull this off.

I hope the others that I did not list individually know how much their support has also meant. Thank you to my friends and family.

Shannon Stiles

25 October 2017

Introduction

The beach and the tropics are two phrases that bring a smile to almost everyone's face. The lapping waves, the fresh ocean breeze, the warm nights and the sunny days are things we all crave. We picture ourselves, lounging in the sun, eating exotic meals, drinking fruity drinks and letting our cares float away.

Why can't we experience some small taste of these dreams every day?

Over the past two decades, I have been lucky enough to spend a good deal of time in the tropics, both working and vacationing. Using my experiences, I've created a cookbook so that we can all bring a small part of these idyllic locations into our daily lives.

Some of the recipes included in Beach Blanket Bistro are traditional foods from tropical countries and beach life; others are inspired by the ingredients and capture the essence of these dream spots. All of them can be created easily in your own kitchen.

I hope you enjoy these dishes as much as I have enjoyed developing them.

For more tips, ideas, and products, please visit **www.beachblanketbistro.com**.

Subscribe to my blog and I'll send you my delicious recipe for **Mango Cannoli**.

Table of Contents

Special Tools

While all these recipes can be made at home with tools found in the standard home kitchen, there are tools mentioned that can make them simpler. As you begin to include the Beach Blanket Bistro meals into your regular dinner rotations, these might be tools to add to your cupboard.

Tortilla Press

These simple presses help make uniform tortillas with little effort. The standard press consists of two round plates, hinged on one side and with a lever handle on the other side. Place a folded piece of wax paper or parchment across the plates, add a ball of dough, close and bring the lever firmly into place. You now have a perfect tortilla ready to hit the skillet, griddle or comal.

Comal

A comal is a round, flat griddle used in Mexico and Central America to primarily cook tortillas. However, they can also be used to sear meat and toast spices.

Zester

While you can zest a piece of citrus with a sharp chef or paring knife, it can be a little dangerous. Scraping away the outside peel of a rounded piece of fruit with a sharp knife is a great way to wind up with a few stitches. I strongly suggest buying a zester.

There are two styles of zester on the market. The first looks like a small hand held grater. The other style has a small handle attached to a piece of metal consisting of a few small rings. The grater style creates finer pieces while the looped style produces small strips. Either works.

Garlic Slicer

Some people like to use a garlic press, but when I was a young man managing a kitchen and housewares store, I fell in love with the garlic slicer/shredders. The small mandolin style slicers have a safe compartment with a small piece of plastic or metal which holds the clove in place without endangering your knuckles. Best of all, it allows you to produce thinly shaved garlic.

Special Ingredients

Banana Leaves

I know there are people out there that are immediately intimidated by the idea of using a banana leaf. Don't be. While it seems exotic, the banana leaf is used around the world. In fact, it is very similar to cooking in parchment paper or in the style called *en papillote*.

People always ask, "Where can I find banana leaves?" The answer is rather simple. You can find them fresh or frozen in most Asian or Latin American markets. Another option is, grow your own. My wife has planted a winter hardy banana varietal (Musa Basjoo) next to our swimming pool and from late spring until the first frost, we use the leaves.

Guava Paste

Guava paste, also known as guayabate, is usually found in large tins or rectangular, plastic wrapped blocks. It is a mixture of pureed guava, sugar and pectin. It can be eaten by itself but is more often used in dishes, either as a solid or liquefied in guava juice or water.

Masa Harina

A type of corn meal mixture. It can be found in the Latin American section of most grocery stores. It is extremely easy to use and should not intimidate the novice.

Yuca

This is a starchy root. It can be found fresh, but most people use the large frozen chunks that can be found in most markets that have a Latin American section.

Cocktails

A good place to start with any gathering is a creative cocktail. Whether it is a celebratory toast, a festive non-alcoholic punch or a simple but strong social lubricant, you can't go wrong.

In this section you will find both the classic concoctions that one would identify with the tropics as well as a few interesting variants that push the palate.

Bottoms Up!

Classic and Strawberry
Mojitos

Simple Syrup

No, simple syrup is not a cocktail. Yes, it is used in many cocktails. Yes, you can buy it.

Now that the questions are answered, here is a simple recipe to make your own. It can be refrigerated in an airtight container for up to two week. I like to prepare a batch once a week and keep it in the refrigerator for drink emergencies.

Yes, there are drink emergencies.

Ingredients

2 cups of granulated sugar

2 cups of water

Preparation

In a sauce pan, heat the sugar and water mixture until the sugar is thoroughly dissolved. Allow to cool and place in an airtight container.

This usually leaves you with about 2/3 of the original volume.

Classic Mojito

The mojito has become a trendy drink in the last decade. Its origin is a mystery. Some claim the history of the mojito goes all the way back to Sir Francis Drake, infamous Elizabethan privateer. The Drake version obviously lacked the effervescence of club soda. Others bring the drink to a more modern origin in the 1930s.

Of course, no matter what the origins the drink, it can't be mentioned without bringing up one of the most famous men to ever promote this Cuban highball, Ernest "Papa" Hemingway. Papa was one of the greatest American authors, adventurers and drinkers to ever live, you know he wouldn't steer you wrong.

Ingredients

½ ounce of fresh squeezed lime juice

3 teaspoons of sugar

5-8 mint leaves

2 ounces of white rum

Club soda

Lime slice for garnish

Preparation

Begin with a highball glass. Muddle the mint leaves (leaving a couple for garnish) with the fresh squeezed lime juice and sugar mixture. Add two ounces of white rum. Stir. Add ice cubes and fill the rest of the glass with club soda. Stir lightly to mix the rum and soda. Garnish with lime and excess mint leaves.

Regarding the mint, what you buy it at the grocery store will most likely be spearmint. Spearmint is commonly used for mojitos, but the ideal is the mojito mint found at some garden supply stores.

Photo on page 10

Strawberry Mojito

As a classic drink becomes re-popularized variations appear. The most popular variation on the Mojito seems to be the strawberry mojito. In keeping with the modern trends, I've included a version of this recipe for those of you who have a berry fetish.

Ingredients

2 medium sized ripe strawberries

½ ounce of fresh squeezed lime juice

3 teaspoons of sugar

5-8 mint leaves (preferably the strawberry mint variant that can be found at garden supply stores)

2 ounces of white rum

Club soda

Preparation

Begin with a highball glass. Muddle the strawberries and mint leaves (leaving a couple for garnish) with the fresh squeezed lime juice and sugar mixture. Add two ounces of white rum. Stir. Add ice cubes and fill the rest of the glass with club soda. Stir lightly to mix the rum and soda. Garnish with excess mint leaves.

Photo on page 10

Basil-Lime Mojito

Another variant that seems to be flourishing is the Basil-Lime Mojito. Basil and lime are natural partners, so it really isn't surprising that this is catching on in some circles.

Ingredients

½ ounce of fresh squeezed lime juice

2 teaspoons of sugar

5-8 basil leaves

2 ounces of white rum

Club soda

Lime slice for garnish

Preparation

Begin with a highball glass. Muddle the basil leaves (leaving a couple for garnish) with the fresh squeezed lime juice and sugar mixture. Add two ounces of white rum. Stir. Add ice cubes and fill the rest of the glass with club soda. Stir lightly to mix the rum and soda. Garnish with lime and excess basil leaves.

Dark and Stormy

This is my favorite drink to deal with the heat of the tropics or a pool party. It has the kick of ginger and the nice mellowness of a good dark rum. Depending on availability of ginger beer, a less flavorful version can be made by substituting ginger ale. I highly recommend that you make the effort to find ginger beer. It is worth it. Trust me.

Ingredients

2 ounces of dark rum (or spiced dark rum)

3 ½ ounces of ginger beer

¼ ounce of fresh lime juice

Lime slice for garnish

Preparation

In a high ball glass, pour the rum over ice. Fill with ginger beer. Add lime juice. Stir. Garnish with lime wedge.

Classic Piña Colada

Many people have told me this drink is too out of date or too much work. I disagree. The Piña Colada is such a classic that you really can't create a beach themed cookbook without including it, nor would I want to do so.

The Piña Colada holds a special place in my heart. The first trip my wife and I took to Costa Rica we stayed at a small hotel that consisted of a tiny but excellent restaurant and ten little ocean view casitas. During our stay, my wife drank more than her fair share of these festive tropical drinks. Occasionally, she would get one that, despite the heavy amount of crushed ice, would be room temperature. It became a mystery I had to solve.

Eventually, when I placed an order at the bar one afternoon, the mystery was solved. The beautiful young bartender opened up the refrigerator, let out an exasperated sigh, grabbed a machete that was hanging behind the bar and disappeared out the backdoor. A few minutes later, she returned with a pineapple, freshly cut from a small patch behind the bar. The drink was warm because the pineapple was still warm from the sun!

Ingredients

2 ½ ounces of white rum

3 ounces of unsweetened pineapple juice or 3 ounces fresh diced pineapple

1 ounce of coconut cream (the sugary sweet cream, not coconut milk)

Pineapple wedge for garnish

Preparation

Mix the ingredients in a blender. As it mixes, drop in 6 to 8 ice cubes. Blend until thick, frothy and smooth. Pour in a glass and turn on some tropical music.

Classic Daiquiri

The Daiquiri is named after a Cuban mine and it has become accepted that the drink owes its origins to a mine engineer named Jennings Cox who created the concoction around the time of the Spanish American War. Over the years his basic recipe evolved to what we now consider the classic daiquiri.

Ingredients

2 ounces of white rum

1 ½ ounces of simple syrup

1 ounce of lime juice

Lime slice for garnish

Preparation

Pour rum, simple syrup and lime juice in a shaker containing four or five ice cubes. Shake vigorously. Strain into a chilled glass. Garnish and serve.

Frozen Strawberry Daiquiri

The most common variant of the daiquiri is, of course, the Frozen Strawberry Daiquiri. This sweet drink has been popularized and is featured at every fern bar in any American town, but this doesn't mean it isn't good. It is especially good when made with fresh berries and good rum.

Ingredients

2 ounces of white rum

2 ounces of simple syrup

1 ounce of lime juice

½ cup of chopped fresh strawberries

½ cup of ice

1 small strawberry for garnish

Preparations

Place all ingredients into a blender. Mix to a slush like consistency. Pour into a tall glass and garnish with a strawberry.

Rum Punch

Rum punch is a vague name at best. In fact, this drink has as many origin stories as it has variations. This is the simplest, and according to many, the original recipe. It even comes with a mnemonic device to help you remember the ingredients. *One sour, two sweet, three strong and four weak.* It sounds odd, but after a couple you will need anything to help you remember the recipe.

Ingredients

½ ounce of lime juice (the sour)

1 ounce of simple syrup (the sweet)

1 ½ ounces of dark rum (the strong)

2 ounces of coconut water (the weak)

Lime slice for garnish

Bitters (if you are feeling suitably colonial)

Preparation

Pour all the ingredients (except the bitters) into a shaker with a few ice cubes. Shake vigorously. Pour over ice in a high ball glass. Optional (add two dashes of bitters). Garnish and serve.

Planters Punch

Like most drinks, there are countless variations on the recipe. Its colorful history is said to have started at the Planter Hotel in South Carolina, but nearly every tiki bar and tropical hotel has their own version.

Ingredients

2 ounces of dark rum

½ ounce of fresh lemon juice

1 ½ ounces of pineapple juice

1 ½ ounces of orange juice

½ ounce of grenadine

3 dashes of bitters

Pineapple wedge for garnish

Preparation

Pour all liquids, except for the bitters into an ice-filled shaker. Shake vigorously. Pour into glass, add bitters and garnish.

Tropical Punch (non-alcoholic)

Since my friends don't want their children drinking my various rum concoctions, I have included a non-alcoholic punch. I suppose rum or vodka could be added to the recipe.

Ingredients

1 pint of mango nectar

1 pint of unsweetened pineapple juice

1 pint of coconut water

2 cups of orange juice

2 -16 ounce bottles of ginger ale

2 cups of diced pineapple

1 sliced orange

Preparation

Add all liquid ingredients into a large punch bowl. Add diced pineapple and sliced orange. Chill.

Appetizers & Small Plates

      I have always been a fan of small plates and appetizers. There is nothing better than getting a small burst of flavor to set the tone for dinner. Of course, these can also be used to create a tapas style dinner party or just providing something unique to absorb the alcohol at a cocktail party.

      If you do serve these at a cocktail party, I suggest you mix and match to give the widest variety. And as I have learned, don't forget to provide at least one vegetarian option.

Shrimp and Palm Heart Salad Salad

Shrimp and Palm Heart Salad

Palm Hearts or *Palmitos* have a delicate flavor, which some people compare to artichoke hearts. In my opinion, palm hearts are more subtle, less fibrous and work with a wider variety of complementary flavors. When added to a salad and paired with shrimp, they give you a nice, light summer appetizer or small meal.

Ingredients

1-14 ounce can of palm hearts

½ pound of small shrimp, peeled

½ pound of baby spinach leaves

1 jalapeño pepper, sliced thin and seeded

¼ cup of olive oil

Juice of 2 tangerines

1 small red onion, sliced

1 tablespoon of white wine vinegar

¼ teaspoon of salt

¼ teaspoon of coarse ground black pepper

Preparation

Boil the shrimp for 2-3 minutes. Place in a bowl of ice to chill. Drain the palm hearts and slice into ¼ inch pieces. Wash and spin the spinach and then divide on four small plates.

Mix olive oil, vinegar and tangerine juice, salt, pepper and jalapeño in a bowl. Add shrimp and let set for 10 minutes. Remove the shrimp and place them on the plates of spinach. Place palm hearts and onion slices on the spinach. Add the oil, tangerine, jalapeño and vinegar mixture as a dressing.

Mango Salsa

This salsa is versatile and refreshing. It can be served with tortilla chips, Tostones (pg 81) or as a sauce for grilled fish, chicken or pork. It is also a main component in the Grilled Swordfish with Mango Salsa recipe (pg 49).

Ingredients

2 medium sized, ripe mangos, peeled and diced

¼ cup of red onion diced

1 jalapeño pepper, finely chopped

2 tablespoons of lemon juice

2 tablespoons of unsweetened pineapple juice

2 tablespoons of chopped mint

¼ teaspoon of salt

Preparation

Mix the mango, onion and pepper in a non-reactive bowl. Muddle half the mint leaves in a mixture of the lemon and pineapple juice. Pour mint and juice mixture over the other ingredients. Stir in salt and remaining mint. Chill for 1 hour.

Classic Guacamole

The noble avocado has an origin going back to the Cenezoic Era when megafauna feasted on the unusual fruit. It survived and changed over the centuries. It was one of the first domesticated fruits in the Western Hemisphere where it became a staple as early as 500 BC. Since the early 20th century, it has been a favorite in the United States; and by the 21st century, it has become a feature at every fast food joint in every town.

But no matter what the uses or origins of the fruit, guacamole is still what most people think of when they hear the word avocado. Unless of course you lived through the 1970s, then avocado is synonymous with the color of kitchen appliances.

Here is a simple, classic guacamole recipe that doesn't require any avocado colored kitchen appliances.

Ingredients

4 medium or large avocados

Juice of 1 lime

1 teaspoon of ground cumin seed

1 teaspoon of garlic powder

½ teaspoon of salt

Preparation

Peel and pit the avocados, retaining one pit. In a medium bowl mash the avocados with the lime juice. Fold in the cumin, garlic powder and salt, being sure to evenly disperse them. Serve with tortilla chips, plantain chips or just eat it as a side dish.

So why retain one pit? Because of a tip I learned from my sister-in-law, April. If you place a whole pit in with the guacamole, it helps keep the avocado from darkening for a short time.

Mango-Serrano Guacamole

Building on a classic is a food tradition. I began to play with the idea of adding additional flavors and textures to guacamole while staying in Playa Guiones, Costa Rica. It started with adding some sliced mango or other readily available tropical fruits. When I returned home, I thought about how well heat and sweet go together. That is when I came up with this sweet and spicy version of guacamole. You will note that I halved the cumin and garlic to allow the sweetness of the mango to shine through.

Ingredients

4 medium or large avocados

2 serrano peppers

1 small ripe mango

Juice of 1 lime

½ teaspoon of ground cumin seed

½ teaspoon of garlic powder

½ teaspoon of salt

Preparation

Peel and dice the mango.

Over an open flame give a quick roast to the serrano peppers. After the pepper cools, scrape off the char, seed and dice them.

Peel and pit the avocados, retaining one pit. In a medium bowl mash the avocados with the lime juice. Mix in the cumin, garlic powder and salt. Gently fold in the diced mango and peppers, evenly dispersing them. Serve with tortilla chips, plantain chips or just eat it as a side dish.

Use the whole avocado pit as a preserving agent.

Chorizo Poppers

The jalapeño popper has become a staple at every run of the mill bar and grill. The reasons for the success of the poppers is simple. They have a touch of heat, a touch of cheese to dull the heat; and they are fun and easy to eat.

The Chorizo Popper is a more complex version that is easily made at home.

Ingredients

6 large jalapeño peppers

1 pound of Mexican style chorizo

½ cup of Queso Chihuahua

½ cup of Queso Fresco

12 strips of bacon

Preparation

Cut the peppers in half. Remove the seeds. Brown the chorizo and drain the excess grease. Let cool. Mix the chorizo, Queso Fresco and Queso Chihuahua in a food processor until evenly blended. Spoon the mixture into the halved peppers. Wrap each stuffed pepper half in one strip of bacon and secure with a toothpick or small skewer.

Broil for 3 to 4 minutes per side or until bacon is cooked.

Olive Tapenade

This is wonderful to serve chilled with some simple, thinly sliced toasted bread, pita or crackers.   After a morning at the beach, my friends and I have made an entire lunch out of this tapenade, some goat cheese, a couple of loaves of bread and a bottle or two of chilled Vinho Verde.

This tapenade can also be used as a great topping for seared rare tuna.

Ingredients

¼ cup of white wine vinegar

Juice of 1 lemon

¼ cup of olive oil

1 tablespoon garlic, finely chopped

2 cups of sliced black olives

2 diced scallions

1 teaspoon of ground cumin seed

Salt (to taste)

Preparation

Whisk the lemon juice, olive oil, vinegar, garlic and cumin together. Add in the olives and scallions. Salt to taste. Let set for 30 minutes. Stir and serve.

Tuna Carpaccio

This tuna dish is simple and yet it impresses. It is also the first of many tuna recipes you will find in this book. As you will discover, I am a huge fan of fresh tuna, particularly yellowfin. I know most tuna connoisseurs rave about bluefin, but I still prefer the yellowfin.   It is versatile, flavorful and a hell of a lot of fun to catch or cheaper to buy. If you don't have the opportunity to catch your own yellowfin, any good, fresh tuna purchased from a fish market works.

Ingredients

1 pound fresh tuna loin

Juice of 2 limes

1 tablespoon of olive oil

1 tablespoon of garlic, chopped

1 ½ tablespoons of capers

Preparation

Using a very sharp knife shave the tuna loin into thin slices. If this is an issue you have two other methods to use. Either partially freeze the loin before slicing, although I do not recommend this as it does change the flavor, or slice thicker slices and place them between two sheets of plastic wrap to pound it thinner.

Place the thin slices on a large serving tray. Drizzle with olive oil and lime juice. Dress with chopped garlic and capers. Chill for 5-10 minutes before serving.

Stuffed Sweet Peppers with Balsamic Reduction

These combine some of my favorite basic ingredients and can be presented beautifully with little effort. They have a sophisticated appearance but require very little work, so they are a perfect summertime party appetizer or a beach picnic addition.

Ingredients

8 mini sweet peppers

1/2 cup of ricotta cheese

½ cup of shredded mozzarella

2 tablespoons of chopped basil leaf

¼ teaspoon of salt

½ cup Balsamic Reduction (pg 101)

Preparation

Wash and stem the peppers, removing the seeds but leaving the peppers as intact as possible. In a small bowl, mix the ricotta, mozzarella, chopped basil and salt until the basil is evenly distributed. Using either a pastry bag (or a more simple makeshift pastry bag fashioned by making a funnel out of wax paper), pipe the cheese filling into the peppers. Place in the refrigerator to chill until ready to serve.

Remove the peppers from the refrigerator. Drizzle with balsamic reduction and serve.

Palm Heart and Cheese Papusas

The papusa, the national dish of El Salvador, is essentially a stuffed, grilled corn tortilla. This is an over simplification, but is still the best way to describe them to anyone who hasn't tried them. They can be an appetizer or a meal.

I first fell in love with these delicious packets of flavor while attending a conference in San Salvador, El Salvador. With two friends of mine, I ditched the standard first night dinner, hopped in a taxi and went to a mom and pop papusa shop. We stuffed ourselves with a variety of papusas and local beer. The food, the people and the atmosphere made the evening for me.

All papusas are traditionally served with Curtido (pg 74). Of course, they are also great all by themselves.

Palm Heart and Cheese Papusas (cont.)

Ingredients

4 cups of masa harina

2 cups of warm water

2 cups of Queso Fresco

2 cloves of garlic

2 tablespoons of chopped chives

1-14 ounce can of palm hearts

1 teaspoon of white pepper

½ teaspoon of salt

2 tablespoons of vegetable oil

Preparation

Filling: In a food processor, puree the palm hearts and garlic. Lower the speed on the processor and add the chives, salt, pepper and cheese. When a firm paste is formed, the filling is ready.

Dough: Gradually add the 2 cups of warm water to the masa harina. Mix the dough by hand. It should be sticky but workable.

Papusa: Form 2- 2 inch ball of dough. Flatten each ball by using a tortilla press or by placing between two sheets of parchment paper and using a rolling pin. Place two tablespoons of filling on one of the flattened rounds. Place the other round on top of the filling. Crimp the edges of the papusa. Place oil in a shallow frying pan and heat. Fry each papusa for three minutes on each side, or until starting to brown.

Beef and Olive Papusas

This version of the beef papusas includes black olives. While not traditional, the salty taste and softer texture of the olives provide a balance to the onion. All papusas are traditionally served with Curtido(pg 74) but don't feel limited in your serving style.

Ingredients

4 cups of masa harina

2 cups of warm water

2 pounds of lean ground beef.

1 medium yellow onion, finely chopped

1 red bell pepper, finely chopped

1 tablespoon of garlic, chopped

½ cup of chopped black olives, drained and rinsed

2 tablespoons of vegetable oil

Preparation

Filling: Heat the vegetable oil on medium heat. Add the onions, pepper and garlic. Heat until the onions turn translucent. Crumble the ground beef into the mixture and brown. Stir in the olive pieces.

Dough: Gradually add the 2 cups of warm water to the masa harina. Mix the dough by hand. It should be sticky but workable.

Papusa: Form 2- 2 inch ball of dough. Flatten each ball by using a tortilla press or by placing between two sheets of parchment paper and flattening. Place two tablespoons of filling on one of the flattened rounds. Place the other round on top of the filling. Crimp the edges of the papusa. Place oil in a shallow frying pan and heat. Fry each papusa for three minutes on each side, or until evenly browned.

Chicken Papusas

While there are traditional chicken papusas, I decided to take this recipe another direction. Think of this particular version as a Latin chicken pot pie.

Ingredients

4 cups of masa harina

2 cups of warm water

4 boneless skinless chicken breasts

2 cups of chicken broth

¼ cup of yellow onion

2 celery stalks, finely chopped

2 teaspoons of ground cumin

1 teaspoon of salt

2 tablespoons of vegetable oil

Preparation

Filling: Boil the chicken breasts in the broth until white and tender enough to shred. In a skillet, heat the olive oil. Sweat the onion and celery until tender. Add the cumin and salt. Stir in the shredded chicken and mix thoroughly.

Dough: Gradually add the 2 cups of warm water to the masa harina and mix by hand.

Papusa: Form 2- 2 inch ball of dough. Flatten each ball by using a tortilla press or by placing between two sheets of parchment paper and flattening. Place two tablespoons of filling on one of the flattened rounds. Place the other round on top of the filling. Crimp the edges of the papusa. Place oil in a shallow frying pan and heat. Fry each papusa for three minutes on each side, or until evenly browned.

Ceviche

Ceviche is the quintessential cool summer appetizer or light meal. Crisp, cold and citrusy. My friends in Latin America also swear that the left over liquid, called Sangre de Tigre (tiger's blood) is a great hangover cure. I may or may not be able to confirm these healing properties.

There are more complicated versions known as ceviche mixto, which include shrimp, baby octopus and scallops, but the simple fish ceviche can't be beat.

Ceviche (cont.)

Ingredients

1 pound of firm white ocean fish. (I prefer sea bass.)

1 small red onion, finely chopped

2 tablespoons of garlic, chopped

2 stalks of celery, finely chopped

2 small serrano peppers finely chopped

2 tablespoons of olive oil

1 cup of lime juice

1 cup of lemon juice

Additional lime and lemon slices for garnish.

Preparation

Dice the fish into bite size pieces. Place the fish, garlic and onion in a large non-reactive bowl or casserole dish. Cover with the lime and lemon juice. Be sure to cover the fish completely with the juice. This ensures the "cooking" with the acidic juices. Refrigerate for at least 4 hours or until the fish is "cooked" through.

Add chopped celery, peppers and olive oil. Chill. Serve in small bowls or martini glasses garnished with additional lime and/or lemon. This can be eaten with tortilla chips, crackers or simply eaten by itself.

Don't forget to drink the Sangre de Tigre for the full effect.

Seafood

While growing up in a landlocked state in the middle of the U.S. I never tasted really fresh seafood. Most of what I had been exposed to was frozen seafood that had been out of the water longer than it had been in the water. To me, everything tasted overly 'fishy" and slightly like a refrigerated tractor trailer. Because of this, I believed I was not a fan of seafood.

As I began to travel to coastal areas, I discovered that I was actually a fan of fresh seafood. Finally, the great secret was revealed to me; loving seafood is about having access to good, fresh seafood.

Returning from waterfront destinations, I began to seek out restaurants with better quality seafood. I started to explore cooking seafood and learned that with faster means of transportations available, more stores were carrying fresher fish.

If possible, it is always better to cook with fresh seafood, the fresher the better. I suggest that if you do not live near the sea, take the time to find a really good fish market.

Herb Encrusted Tuna Loin

A ten minute recipe that seems like you spent hours preparing and planning, combined with my favorite fish. What could be better? The preparation of the herbs is the most time consuming thing about this recipe, but with a food processor even that takes no time at all.

Ingredients

4 pieces of tuna loin or 1 inch thick tuna steaks

¼ cup of rosemary

¼ cup of oregano

¼ cup of thyme

2 cloves of garlic

½ teaspoon of salt

Zest of 1 lemon

½ teaspoon of olive oil

Preparation

Place the herbs, garlic and lemon zest in a food processor. Grind the spices, then add the olive oil to create a paste. Coat the tuna in the rub by gently pushing the rub into the steaks. Sear the steaks in a hot nonstick skillet for about 2 minutes on each side for rare tuna.

Grilled Lobster Tails with Garlic-Chive Butter

Everyone loves lobster. If they say otherwise they have never tried it. Lobster is not a complicated thing to cook, and grilled lobster is one of the easiest meals on the planet. Unless, of course, you have to catch the lobster yourself.

Ingredients

4 lobster tails

½ cup of salted butter

1 tablespoon olive oil

2 cloves of shaved or finely sliced garlic

2 tablespoon chopped chives

¼ teaspoon of salt

Preparation

Melt the butter slowly over low heat. Stir in the garlic, chives and salt.

Use cooking sheers to butterfly the lobster tails. Be sure to cut along on the underside. Using skewers to hold open the tail, place them cut side down on the grill over medium-high heat. Grill for 6 minutes or until shell turn red.

Turn the tails over and heavily drizzle the inside with the garlic-chive butter. Grill for 2 to 3 minutes or until the flesh is firm and white.

Dorado in Banana Leaf

Dorado in Banana Leaf

Dorado is called by many names depending on where you live and who runs the fish market you frequent. It is commonly called by the Hawaiian name, Mahi Mahi, as well as the unfortunate name of Dolphinfish and Shiira by the Japanese. It is one of the fastest growing fish in the ocean and is prolific so there is little worry about over fishing. It is very mild and is great served in a variety of ways, but this is definitely one of my favorite styles in which to cook this wonderful fish.

The presentation of this dish makes it great for small dinner parties or impressing a date. I suggest pairing it with Coconut Rice (pg 76).

Ingredients

4- 4 ounce pieces of dorado

4 squares of banana leaf – washed and patted dry

4 small sweet red peppers

1 ounce of fresh ginger

2 medium shallots

4 cups of coconut milk

8 piece of cooking twine

1 tablespoon of vegetable oil

1 tablespoon of black pepper

1 teaspoon of salt

1 teaspoon of white pepper

(continued on next page)

Photo on previous page

Dorado in Banana Leaf (cont.)

Preparation

Seed and julienne the red pepper. Dice the shallots. Slice the ginger. Place one piece of dorado in the center of each banana leaf square. Evenly distribute the julienned peppers on top of each piece of dorado. Dust with black pepper and salt. Fold the banana leaves into tight packets and tie with the cooking twine.

Heat the oil in a pan. Add the banana leaf packets of dorado and pepper. Seer each side for 2-3 minutes. Pour the coconut milk, shallots and ginger over the packets. Simmer for 10-12 minutes.

Remove the packets. Pour the coconut mixture into blender to create a smooth sauce. Open the packets of fish and pour a small amount of coconut mixture over the fish and serve.

Barbecued Shrimp Skewers

I love barbecued shrimp, but the secret to shrimp on the grill is not overcooking them. If this recipe was for plain grilled shrimp, I would recommend leaving the shells on, this usually allows a little more leeway in cooking times and provides a richer flavor. However, when using a sauce or baste, I prefer to peel the shrimp before they hit the grill. The sauce adds a new level of taste and keeps the shrimp from drying out.

One note on serving sizes. Between 7 and 10 large shrimp is a good entrée serving size. Of course, this leads to another issue, shrimp sizes are not uniform, so always go by the per pound count. For "large" shrimp I would recommend a count of 31-35 per pound.

Ingredients

1 pound of large shrimp, peeled

2 tablespoons of olive oil

1 cup of Guava Chipotle Barbecue Sauce (pg 105)

Preparations

Place the shrimp on skewers lengthwise, tip to tail, leaving no space between each shrimp, but not crowding them. If you are using bamboo skewers remember to soak them in water for at least 30 minutes before skewering the shrimp. This keeps the skewers from becoming so much kindling.

Lightly brush the shrimp with olive oil. Place on a hot grill. Grill for about 1 minute of each side. Using about half of the sauce, baste and grill for about 1 minute more on each side. Serve with extra sauce on the side.

Creole Shrimp

This recipe has a bit of French Caribbean influence. There is almost a Cajun feel to the recipe, but it also is reminiscent of Cuban and Haitian dishes. It works well when served over plain rice, but if served with the Mojito Rice (pg 86) it adds another layer of flavor.

Ingredients

2 pounds of shelled and deveined "large" shrimp

4 roma tomatoes, chopped

½ cup celery, chopped

½ cup yellow onion, diced

1 tablespoon of minced garlic

3 tablespoons of olive oil

½ teaspoon of cayenne pepper

½ teaspoon of salt

½ teaspoon brown sugar

¼ dry white wine

Preparation

Heat the olive oil on medium. Add the onion, celery, garlic, tomato, sugar and spices. Sweat the mixture for approximately 4 minutes or until the celery and onion begins to become tender. Add the shrimp and cook for 4 more minutes. While stirring, add the wine and cook for three minutes.

Grilled Swordfish with Mango Salsa

The firmness of swordfish makes it one of my favorite fish to grill. It cooks fast, stays firm and is very versatile. There is something special about swordfish. It has such a mild taste that it can be spiced and accented to make so many great dishes.

Here it is dressed with the Mango Salsa (pg 24), but it is also great with the Mojo (pg 107) or the Olive Tapenade (pg 30).

Ingredients

4-1 inch thick swordfish steaks

1 tablespoon of vegetable oil

4 fresh pineapple rings

½ teaspoon of coarse ground black pepper

¼ teaspoon of salt

2 cups of Mango Salsa (pg 24)

Preparations

Bring your grill to medium high heat. Lightly brush the swordfish with the oil. Season with black pepper and salt. Place the swordfish on the grill. Grill the fish for about 5-7 minutes per side, turning once. Add the pineapple to the grill. Grill the pineapple rings just enough to add caramel colored grill marks.

When plating, stack each fish portion on top of a pineapple ring. Top with the mango salsa.

Poke

This Hawaiian tuna dish is popular just about everywhere. While my first experience with this dish was at a small stand on Maui, I have also had it at an eco-lodge in Costa Rica, a seafood restaurant in southern California and bought some at an upscale grocer outside of St. Louis, Missouri.

Some of the different versions contain ingredients that are difficult to find away from the coast or larger cities, but this version can be made with ingredients found at most grocers.

Ingredients

2 pounds of fresh tuna steaks

1 cup of green onions, chopped

¼ ounce of grated ginger

½ cup of soy sauce

1 tablespoon of crushed red pepper flakes

2 tablespoons of sesame oil

1 tablespoon of toasted sesame seeds

Preparation

Dice the tuna into 1 inch cubes. Place the tuna, green onions and pepper flakes in a non-reactive bowl. In another bowl, whisk the sesame oil, soy sauce and ginger. Pour the liquid over the tuna, onion pepper mixture. Toss and garnish with sesame seeds. Refrigerate for three hours.

Tropical Lobster Roll

Lobster rolls can traditionally be found in two styles; the Maine and Connecticut versions. The Maine consists of cold lobster salad served on a long thin bun and the Connecticut is lobster pieces served warm in garlic butter and placed on grilled bread.

I was inspired by tropical flavors and my love of lobster to create this roll. The buttery flavor of the lobster blends with the mojo sauce, tropical fruits and vegetables to create something different.

Ingredients

2 lobster tails

¼ cup of Mojo (pg 24)

¼ cup of mango, diced

1 thinly serrano pepper, sliced and seeded

2 tablespoons of minced red onion

4 Hawaiian rolls

Preparation

Use cooking sheers to butterfly the lobster tails, cut on the underside. Using skewers to hold open the tail, place them cut side down on the grill over medium-high heat. Grill for 6 minutes or until shell turn red. Turn and grill for 2 to 3 minutes or until the flesh is firm and white.

Remove the meat from the lobster tails and set aside in a non-reactive bowl.

Toss lobster with the mango, pepper and onion. Add Mojo and refrigerated for 1 to 2 hours. Spoon into split Hawaiian rolls and serve.

Moqueca, Brazilian Fish Stew

This stew uses a coconut milk base and has a flavor that just screams beach food. Any firm white fish can be used but I prefer sea bass. The real trick is to not overcook the fish. You want it to stay firm and not just flake away.

With a little samba in the background, you'll start to believe you are in Brazil.

Ingredients

2 pounds of firm white fish, preferably sea bass or even sword fish

½ pound of shelled and deveined "large" shrimp

1 tablespoon of minced garlic

¼ cup of lime juice

¼ cup green onions, chopped

2 yellow bell peppers, diced

1 tablespoon of sweet paprika

2 teaspoons of crushed red pepper flakes

2 tablespoons of cilantro, chopped

1-14 ounce can of coconut milk

2 tablespoons of olive oil

Preparation

Cut the fish into 3 inch portions. Place in a non-reactive dish. Pour the lime juice and garlic over the fish and let rest for 30 minutes.

In a small stock pot, heat the olive oil. Add the onions and peppers to the hot oil. Sweat the mixture for 10 to 20 minutes. Add the marinated fish on top of the mixture. Spoon about ¼ of the mixture over the fish. Add the shrimp, paprika, pepper flakes and cilantro. Pour in the coconut milk and simmer for 15 minutes.

Ridiculously Easy Tuna Salad

At times in Costa Rica, I have caught enough yellowfin tuna that it became difficult to decide what to do with it all. It has never been a large enough quantity to go through the hassle of trying to bring it back to the U.S., but it has often been enough to need new ways to eat it.

This recipe does something that I never thought I would do much less recommend...use a microwave in real cooking.

Ingredients

1 pound of fresh tuna

2 tablespoons of water

¼ cup of green onions, chopped

2 tablespoons of Greek yogurt

1 tablespoon of dill, chopped

4 sweet pickles, chopped

Preparation

Cut the tuna into ¾ inch cubes. Place in a small bowl with the water and cover with plastic wrap. Microwave on high for 1 minute or until tuna is steamed white. Allow the tuna to cool. Shred the tuna.

In a second bowl mix the green onion, dill, yogurt and pickles. Add the shredded tuna. Mix.

Meats & Poultry

For some reason, many people tend to disregard red meat when thinking about beach food. I have never quite understood this. Some of the best beef and pork I have eaten has been in the tropics. My favorite steakhouse in the world isn't found in the Plains States in the US, it is less than two miles from the ocean in Panama City, Panama.

In the same vein, my favorite pork dishes originate in Cuba and Puerto Rico.

Most people do not think of pork when they think of the Caribbean, however, pork is much more common than beef. Islands tend to use smaller animals for food, due to the lack of space. So one of the best places to find pork dishes are going to be on small tropical islands.

Chickens also fit into the small animal category. It is pretty hard to find a location you cannot raise chickens. They also reproduce rather quickly, so the supply never runs low.

Grilled BBQ Pork

Grilled Barbecue Pork Medallions with Fire Roasted Peppers

Although I also like butterfly cut pork chops, using a nice center cut pork tenderloin and cutting your own medallions is my favorite way to cook pork. This allows you to cut the thickness you desire and allows for portion control.

Any type of pepper works with this dish, I prefer the small sweet peppers, but you could easily substitute jalapeño or poblanos.

Ingredients

1-1 pound center cut pork loin

8 small sweet peppers

2 cups of Guava Chipotle Barbecue Sauce

Preparation

Slice the tenderloin into 1 inch this medallions or chops. Using a grill with two different heats set on each side. Grill the chops for 2 minutes on the high heat, turning once. Move the chops to the cooler side and grill for 5 minutes turning once. Brush with the sauce and grill for 3 more minutes, turning once. Repeat. Internal temperature should be 145 degrees Fahrenheit or 65 degrees Celsius.

Jerk Chicken Kebabs

While you can use the Jerk Marinade (pg 106) on a whole chicken or on various pieces, I am a huge fan of kebabs. Meat on a stick might be the greatest of mankind's inventions. It is portable, easy to eat and you can dress them up with any assortment of vegetables if you so choose.

When it comes to dressing a Jerk Kebab, pineapple is the way to go. In this recipe, it really brings out the additional sweetness of the marinade and gives a great contrast to the onion.

Ingredients

4 boneless skinless chicken breasts

1 cup of Jerk Marinade (pg 106)

1 red onion

1 small pineapple

Preparation

Cut the boneless chicken breasts into 1 ½ cubes. Place in a sealable plastic bag with the 1 cup of Jerk Marinade. Massage to fully coat the chicken. Refrigerate for a minimum of 2 hours.

Cut the pineapple into 1 to 2 inch cubes. Slice the red onion into large petals.

Skewer the sliced onion, pineapple and chicken on to skewers. Grill on medium heat for 12 minutes, rotating for even cooking.

Steak Tampiqueña Rolls

While I was working on several other recipes and testing them on family and friends, my brother mentioned steak tampiqueña on multiple occasions. I didn't want to just throw in an average tampiqueña recipe, so I tried to come up with an homage.

After several false starts, I decided to use the steak as the foundation for a completely different style of recipe. This is in no way traditional, but it is tasty.

So, Shawn, here is your tampiqueña type recipe.

Ingredients

4- 8 ounce sirloins, thin cuts

2 tablespoons of garlic, chopped

2 tablespoons of ground cumin

Juice of 3 limes

8 to 10 baby spinach leaves per steak

1 cup of the filling from the Palm Heart and Cheese Papusa recipe (pg 34)

Preparation

Place each steak between two pieces of wax paper. Using the flat side of a meat tenderizer, flatten each to ¼ inch thickness or thinner if possible.

Whisk the garlic and cumin into the lime juice. Marinate the steaks in this juice mixture for 1 to 2 hours.

Remove the steaks from the marinade. Pat dry. Line each steak with a single layer of spinach leaves. Spread a thin layer of cheese mixture on the spinach leaves. Roll the steak and either tie with cooking twine or use bamboo skewers to hold the rolls together

Grill on medium high heat until the reach desired level of color.

Jerk Pork Chops

The jerk marinade is great on pork. The combination of heat and sweetness brings out the full flavor of good pork.

The secret to grilling these chops is using both indirect and direct heat. Keeping one side of your grill hotter while allowing the other to have a lower flame works great when dealing with difficult meats like pork. Sear first on the high heat then slow cook on the cooler side. It allows you to lock in the juices while still cooking the pork effectively.

Ingredients

4 butterfly pork chops- ¾ inch thick

2 cups of Jerk Marinade (pg 106)

1 lime (for garnish)

Preparation

Wash and pat dry the pork chops. Place into a clean sealable bag. Pour in the Jerk Marinade. Massage the bag the evenly distribute the marinade. Refrigerate for 4 hours.

Using a grill with two different heats set on each side. Grill the chops for 2 minutes on the high heat, turning once. Move the chops to the cooler side and grill 10 minutes turning once. Internal temperature should be 145 degrees Fahrenheit or 65 degrees Celsius.

Slow Cooked Chicken Tacos

This simple dish is just spicy slow cooked chicken shredded and put on fresh flour tortillas. Add a little Curtido (pg 74) and Queso Fresco.

Ingredients

Chicken:

1 ½ pounds boneless, skinless chicken breasts, thighs or a mix

½ cup of dry vermouth

2 large dried ancho peppers

2 tablespoons of ground cumin

2 tablespoons garlic, finely chopped

1 cup of water

1 teaspoon of salt

Flour Tortilla:

4 cups all-purpose flour

1 teaspoon of salt

2 teaspoons of baking powder

2 tablespoons of shortening or lard

1 ½ cups of warm water

Condiments:

1 cup of Curtido (pg 74)

¼ cup of Queso Fresco

60

Preparation

Chicken: Place the ancho peppers in a heat resistant bowl. Add 1 cup of boiling water. Let set for 20 minutes. Remove the peppers from the water and slice into strips, discarding the stems. Place the chicken in a baking dish or roaster. Add the peppers and the water. Add the wine, cumin, garlic and salt. Cover with aluminum foil or the roaster lid. Bake at 350 degrees for 2 hours. Shred the chicken, then place it back in the liquid and let set for 5 minutes.

Tortillas: Mix the flour, salt and baking powder. Form a mound of the dry ingredients leaving a hollow spot. Pour the water and add the shortening/lard into the open spot. Knead the ingredients until smooth. Form the dough into evenly sized balls and roll flat with a floured rolling pin or use a tortilla press. Place the tortillas in a hot greased skillet or use a comal to cook them. Turn them once, when the top begins to have a sheen.

Place the chicken into the warm tortillas, top with a tablespoon of Curtido and sprinkle with Queso Fresco.

Chicken Milanesa

Chicken Milanesa are common in many areas of Latin America. This particular version includes the use Mojo (pg 107) as a marinade. This gives it a more complex flavor, combining a hint of citrus and peppers to the chicken.

Ingredients

4 boneless, skinless chicken breast

1 cup Mojo (pg 107)

3 cups of plain bread crumbs

2 cups of flour

3 eggs

2 cups of vegetable oil

2 teaspoons of black pepper

2 teaspoons of salt

1 teaspoon of smoked paprika

½ tablespoon of garlic powder

½ tablespoon of crushed red pepper flakes

Preparation

Place each chicken breast between two sheets of wax paper and using the flat side of a tenderizing hammer pound flat. Ideally, the thickness should be ¼ inch or less.

Place the breasts in a sealable plastic baggie and cover with the Mojo. Allow the chicken to marinate for at least three hours in the refrigerator.

Mix the paprika, garlic powder, and red pepper flakes into the bread crumbs.

Remove the chicken from the marinade and pat dry.

(continued on next page)

Chicken Milanesa (cont.)

Whisk the eggs and pour into a shallow dish. Mix the salt pepper and flour in another dish. Place the bread crumb mixture in a third dish.

Heat the vegetable oil in a large skillet, to about 375 degrees.   Dredge each piece of chicken in the flour. Dip each in the egg mixture and then coat in the bread crumbs.

Fry each piece of chicken for 3 minutes per side or until golden. Place on a plate lined with paper towels to remove the excess oil.

Picadillo

This dish is common in many parts of Latin America, but my favorite is closer to the Cuban style. Essentially this is simply a hash. Using ground beef for a base, you dress it up with peppers, spices and condiments. This version of the recipe has its roots in the picadillos I've had in Miami, but also has a nod to one I had in eastern Mexico. Traditionally it is served with white rice.

Ingredients

2 pounds of ground beef

1 yellow onion, finely chopped

2 tablespoons garlic, finely chopped

1 tablespoon of ground cumin

2 tablespoons of tomato paste

4 orange sweet peppers, sliced and seeded

4 red sweet peppers, sliced and seeded

2 tablespoons of capers

1 cup of green olives stuffed with pimentos

Juice of 1 Lime

½ cup dry red wine

Preparation

Using a large skillet with a lid. Sweat the peppers, onions and garlic with the cumin. Crumble the ground beef into the vegetable mixture and brown. Stir in the tomato paste, lime juice and red wine. Add capers and olive. Cover and simmer for 10 minutes.

Ropa Vieja

Ropa Vieja is one of the all-time great Cuban dishes. The name literally translates as old clothes, since the long strands of beef mixed with peppers and onions is supposed to resemble a pile of old rags. I know the description isn't all that appetizing, but trust me, it is delicious. Serve this with some Tostones (pg 81), rice and a mojito (pg 12) and you can't go wrong.

Traditionally, this dish is made with the toughest, stringiest cuts of beef, but you can use a flank steak or a chuck roast.

Ingredients

3 pounds of beef (see options above)

1-8 ounce can of tomato paste

1 cup of dry red wine

2 medium yellow onions, quartered

6 bell peppers of assorted colors or 1 ½ pounds of mini sweet peppers

2 tablespoons of ground cumin

2 tablespoons of garlic, finely chopped

2 teaspoons of salt

Preparation

Stem and seed the peppers. Slice into wide strips. Separate the petals from the quartered onion. Using half of the peppers and onions line the bottom of the roaster. Lay the beef on top of the layer of peppers and onions. Mix the cumin, garlic, salt and tomato paste. Pour over the beef. Place the second half of the peppers and onions on top of the meat. Add the red wine. Slow cook at 350 degrees for 4 to 5 hours.

When fork tender, pull the beef apart into long strips.

Mojo Pork Loin

Mojo and pork, are a great combination. The sweet and spicy mojo flavors really compliment pork and any marinade combined with indirect/ direct cooking keeps pork from drying out.

Ingredients

1- pound pork loin

1 cup of Mojo (pg 107) (for marinade)

½ cup of Mojo (pg 107) for topping

1 large orange (for garnish)

Preparation

Place the pork loin between to sheets of plastic wrap or wax paper. Using the smooth side of a meat tenderizing mallet flatten the tenderloin to a ¼ to ½ inch thickness.

Place the tenderloin in a large freezer bag and add the Mojo. Marinate for at least 4 hours in the refrigerator.

Remove the tenderloin from the marinade. Pat dry. Using a grill with two different heats set on each side. Grill the tenderloin for 2 minutes on the high heat, turning once. Move the meat to the cooler side and grill 10 minutes turning once. Internal temperature should be 145 degrees Fahrenheit or 65 degrees Celsius.

Serve with a garnish of thick orange slices and top with the Mojo that had been set aside.

Skirt Steak with Chimichurri

Skirt steak appears to be the steak of choice in many Central American steakhouses and it is impossible to find a steakhouse in Latin America that doesn't have some style of chimichurri. So here is my take on the combination.

For a complete menu, I have served this over Pureed Yuca with Goat Cheese and Garlic (pg 88) and a side of Asparagus with Spanish Chorizo (pg 73).

Ingredients

2 pound skirt steak

2 cups of Chimichurri (pg 102)

Salt and Pepper (to taste)

Preparation

Set aside ½ cup of chimichurri for a steak sauce. Marinate the skirt steak in a 1 ½ cups of the chimichurri.   I prefer to do this by placing the steak in to a sealable plastic bag, cover it in the marinade and massage it assure equal coverage. Refrigerate for a minimum of two hours.

Remove the steak from the marinade and salt and pepper if desired. DO NOT pat dry. Grill over high heat for 6 to 8 minutes, turning once. When removed from grill let set 3 to 5 minutes.

Beef Stuffed Onions

I know this sounds like an odd recipe. Many people are afraid that the onion flavor will be to over powering, but parboiling the onion and then baking them in the tomato sauce makes them very sweet and soft.

Ingredients

4 medium sweet yellow onions

1 pound of ground beef

2 tablespoons of ground cumin

2 tablespoons of garlic, finely chopped

1 teaspoon of salt

1 habanero pepper, stemmed

2 cups of tomato sauce

2 teaspoons of sugar

4 ounces of Queso Chihuahua, shredded

1 cup dry red wine

4 cups of water

Preparation

Slice both ends off of each onion and remove the outer skin. In a large pan, bring the 4 cups of water to a boil. Drop the onions in for 1 to 2 minute to parboil them. Remove the onions and let them cool.

Core each onion removing about ½ of the onion from the center. Dice the cores.

Mix the diced onion cores, the ground beef, 1 tablespoon of ground cumin, 1 tablespoon of the garlic and 1 teaspoon of salt. Brown the mixture.

Fill each onion with a portion of the beef mixture. (continued on next page)

Place the tomato sauce, 1 tablespoon of ground cumin, 1 tablespoon of garlic, red wine and habanero pepper in a blender. Mix thoroughly.

Place the filled onions in a 9 x 9 baking dish. Cover with the tomato sauce. Place in a 350 degree preheated oven for twenty minutes. Add the shredded cheese on each onion. Replace in oven until the cheese is melted.

Side Dishes

What you serve with an entrée makes a world of difference. The flavors and textures of the dishes need to work with one another. At times, they need to both compliment and contrast with each other. I have suggested several pairings in the text and a few of the pictures show *my* ideal pairings.

My suggestion is to experiment. See which combinations work for your palate and what works for your guests' palates.

Asparagus with Spanish Chorizo

As a child I was never fond of vegetables, but I also was something of a burgeoning foodie, before people were actually called "foodies". My mother convinced me to try many foods, but especially asparagus, by telling me it was too expensive and too fancy to waste on children. Needless to say, I decided to eat asparagus and it quickly became my favorite vegetable. This recipe, is a continuation of that love of asparagus.

It is important to note the differences between Spanish and Mexican chorizo. Spanish chorizo tends to be more like a small salami, while Mexican chorizo is ground meat with spices.

Ingredients

4 ounces of dry Spanish chorizo

1 pound of thin or pencil asparagus

2 cloves garlic, thinly sliced

2 tablespoons of olive oil

Juice of ¼ of a lemon

Preparation

Wash the asparagus and remove the woody ends. Steam the asparagus until it satrts to becomestender. This will vary with the thickness of the asparagus.

Thinly slice the chorizo.

In a skillet, heat the olive oil and add the sliced chorizo. Cook, the chorizo over medium heat until the edges begin to curl. Add the garlic. Sautee for 2 minutes. Add the asparagus for 1 minute. Remove from heat. Squeeze lemon juice over asparagus.

Curtido

This spicy Salvadoran slaw is traditionally served with hot papusas. In fact, the first time I ate papusas was also the first time I tried curtido. The peppery heat combined with the sour hooked me on the first bite.

It can also be served with any variety of dishes. My favorite pairing, besides papusas, is with any pork dish.

Ingredients

1 head of cabbage, shredded

2 carrots, shredded

1 small yellow onion, finely sliced

½ cup of white wine vinegar

2 tablespoons of vegetable oil

½ teaspoon of salt

1 sliced habanero pepper

Juice of 1 lemon

Preparation

Combine all ingredients in a non-reactive bowl. Toss. Refrigerate for at least 4 hours. Toss and serve.

Ginger Slaw

The recipe was inspired by the amount of Asian fusion I have found in Central American restaurants, particularly in Panama. Panama has some of the best Asian food I have encountered. Part of the reason for this is the fact that Panama City is home to the oldest China Town in the Americas. Another reason is that 1 in 4 Panamanians have some Chinese ancestry.

Ginger Slaw is a great addition to many meals. In the summer heat, the crisp coldness of a slaw is nice and light. As a slaw, it pairs nicely with the Barbecued Pork Medallions (pg 55) but it is also great with seafood or poultry.

Ingredients

1 ounce finely chopped fresh ginger

1 ½ ounces of soy sauce

Juice of 1 small lime

2 ounces of vegetable oil

1 tablespoon of white wine vinegar

1 medium head of cabbage, shredded

3 small sweet peppers

Pinch of sugar

¼ cup of plain pepitas

Preparation

Mix the ginger. sugar and liquid ingredients in a non-reactive bowl. Let stand for 1 hour to allow the flavors to marry. Shred the cabbage. Slice the peppers into thin rings and add them to the cabbage. Toss the peppers and cabbage with the soy-ginger mixture. Add a generous handful of pepitas. Chill.

Coconut Rice with Grilled Pineapple

Coconut rice can be made to be either sweet or savory. Choosing which style to include in this cookbook was difficult. As the great Jimmy Buffet once said, "Indecision may or may not be my problem." So this version meets somewhere in the middle. Friends have compared it to Thai food and even a risotto.

Ingredients

2 cups of rice (I like to use basmati to give a stickier consistency)

5 cups of coconut milk

1 ounce of shredded or pureed ginger

Juice of 1 lime

1 tablespoon of cream of coconut (the sweet type used in piña coladas)

3- ½ inch thick fresh pineapple rings

2 tablespoons of unsweetened shredded coconut

Preparation

Bring 4 ½ cups of coconut milk to a boil. Reserve ½ cup in a separate bowl. Add rice to the boiling coconut milk. Bring the rice and coconut milk back to a boil, reduce the heat, cover and simmer for 25 minutes or until rice is tender. In the bowl containing the reserve coconut milk, stir in the coconut cream, lime juice and ginger.

Grill or broil the 3 pineapple rings until golden. Let cool and dice them.

Toast the shredded coconut in a small skillet, until golden brown. This happens quickly so be careful not to burn it.

When the rice is tender, remove from heat. Mix in the lime, ginger and coconut mixture. Replace lid and let set for 5 minutes. Stir in the toasted coconut and pineapple.

Black Beans

Beans are another universal food and black beans are arguably the favorite type of bean to use. In my house, there is no arguing the fact, the black bean is the undisputed king of beans. They can be served alone or in combination with white rice. As it is presented ,this is a vegetarian version, however smoked meats and stock can be used in conjunction to make a soup. They can also be mashed and refried.

But the simply seasoned black bean is still my favorite.

Ingredients

1 pound black beans, rinsed thoroughly

1 small yellow onion, chopped

6 cloves of garlic, sliced

2 teaspoons of cumin

1 teaspoon of salt

1 red bell pepper, diced

2 tablespoons of olive oil

Preparation

Overnight soak the beans in 10 cups of water. Drain the beans and replace the water. Add the salt and onion. Bring to a boil. Add the spices and vegetables and let simmer for 1 hour.

Tomato and Zucchini Salad

After a trip to San Diego, I was inspired to create this salad. One of the things that amazed me about the area was the variety of seafood and abundance of very fresh produce. The idea for this salad actually came from overhearing two women discussing using the extra vegetables that they had grown in an urban garden. It so happens that zucchini is always one of those vegetables that gardeners seem to almost overproduce.

The secret to this salad is not using zucchini that are too large. As zucchini get bigger, they tend to become tougher and "woodier". I suggest using small or small-medium size zucchini. This means try to choose the squash that is under 8 inches.

This salad compliments a simple grilled or broiled white fish.

Ingredients

5 Roma tomatoes

3 small to medium zucchini

1 small red onion

2 tablespoons of extra-virgin olive oil

2 tablespoons of red wine vinegar

2 teaspoons of chopped oregano

¼ teaspoon of salt

Preparation

Quarter the Roma tomatoes. Dice the zucchini into ¼ inch pieces. Slice the red onion into rings. Place the zucchini, tomatoes and onion in a non-reactive bowl. In another bowl, whisk the olive oil and vinegar, adding the oregano and salt.

Add the liquid mixture to the other bowl and lightly toss. Chill and serve.

Tostones (patacones)

Tostones are twice fried green plantain. They tend to be a staple in many Latin American countries. However, the name can vary depending on your location. Several areas, including parts of Peru and Costa Rica, call them patacones. Either way, I call them delicious. While they are perfect as a side with just about any meal, don't limit their use. They are great as chip substitutes with Guacamole (pg 25) and are delicious with the Curry Dipping Sauce (pg 103).

Ingredients

2 green plantain

1 cup of vegetable oil

½ teaspoon of salt

Preparation

Peel the green plantain. It is important that the plantain be as unripe as possible. The riper they become, the softer and sweeter they become. Slice the plantain into 1 ½ inch portions.

Heat the oil in a large skillet over medium heat. The oil temperature should be about 300 degrees.

Lightly fry the plantain. Turning to brown evenly.

Remove them from the skillet. Place them on a dish lined with paper towels, allowing them to cool and removing the excess oil. Once cooled, place between two sheets of wax paper and flatten with the bottom of a glass or the palm of your hand.

Turn the heat up on the oil, bringing it to about 375 degrees. Place them back in the hot oil for a second round of frying. Remove them when they turn a golden brown and drain on paper towels. Salt lightly.

Whole Grilled Plantain

Plantain is one of the most versatile foods. You literally can use it in hundreds of dishes. It is a staple in most of the Caribbean and huge swaths of Latin America. This is a great recipe for a barbecue side dish that will surprise your friends.

Ingredients

4 green plantains

½ cup of Balsamic Reduction (pg 101)

2 ounces of orange juice

Preparation

Wash the four plantain. Place them on the grill, making sure there is space between them. This is where patience comes into play. Leave them alone. Turn them once to allow even heating, but leave them on the grill until they turn black and the peel splits open.

While the plantain are grilling. Heat the orange juice in a small sauce pan, stirring in the balsamic.

When the plantain split. Remove from the grill. Widen the opening and drizzle the plantain flesh with the balsamic reduction and orange juice mixture.

Maduros

Unlike the other two recipes using plantain, for this one you want ripe plantain. You can use the yellow ones that are heavily spotted with brown and black, but the darker the plantain the sweeter the end result.

Much like tostones (pg. 81) these are extremely common in Latin or Caribbean meals. In fact, to me, no Cuban or Central American meal would seem complete without a healthy portion of maduros.

Ingredients

2 very ripe plantain

¼ cup of vegetable oil

Preparation

Peel the ripe plantain. Again I cannot stress the importance of them being ripe. Slice the plantain on a diagonal making each piece about 1 inch thick.

In a large skillet bring the oil to about 350 degrees. Place the plantain in the skillet, spaced to allow the best caramelization. Allow each piece to cook for 1 to 2 minutes on each side.

Broiled Stuffed Tomatoes

One of my favorite restaurants in Costa Rica serves a broiled tomato as a side with every meal. It surprised me just how much flavor you could get from a tomato by adding just a little salt and olive oil then tossing it in the broiler.

Building on that foundation I started experimenting with different types of tomatoes and spices. Eventually I settled on my favorite tomato the Roma or Plum tomato. I also like to experiment with textures and ways to limit acidity, so I came up with this version of the broiled tomato.

Tip: Try using a muffin tin or ramekins, they help keep the tomatoes up right.

Ingredients

4 Roma tomatoes

4 ounces of goat cheese

1 tablespoon of chopped oregano

¼ teaspoon of salt

1 tablespoon of olive oil

Preparation

Thoroughly mix the goat cheese, salt and oregano. Remove the tops of the tomatoes and with a paring knife gently remove the pulp and a small amount of the "meat" of the tomatoes. Fill each tomato with about 1 ounce of the mixture. Brush with olive oil.

Broil for 4 minutes, or until the cheese starts to brown.

Mojito Rice

Rice seems to be a universal dish, a blank culinary slate. You can dress it up a thousand different ways to make it interesting or simply serve it as a base layer for another dish. Many cultures have added mint and lime to rice, it really isn't anything new, no matter how clever I thought I was when I decided to try it.

In honor of one of my favorite drinks, the Mojito (pg 12) I have dubbed this version, Mojito Rice. I find that it pairs well with Picadillo (pg 65) or the Steak Tampiqueña Rolls (pg 58).

Ingredients

2 cups of white long grain rice

4 cups of water

1 lime

¼ cup of fresh mint leaves

Preparation

Bring the 4 cups of water to a boil and stir in the rice. Reduce to a simmer and let cook for 20 minutes or until rice is tender. Juice and zest the lime. Roll the mint leaves and slice into very thin strips. While the rice is still warm add the lime juice, zest and mint. Cover and let stand for 10 minutes. Fluff the rice and serve.

Boiled Yuca with Mojo

Yuca or cassava root is common in many areas of the tropics. Many people consider it to be similar to the potato, but I have never been a fan of this description. They are both essentially roots and are great vehicles for other flavors but yuca has a texture that is nothing like a potato. It is more fibrous. It also is much more flavorful than the average potato. This is the first of three recipes that use yuca.

Ingredients

1 pound of frozen yuca

1 tablespoon of salt

1 cup of Mojo (Pg 107)

Preparation

Cover the frozen yucca pieces with 2-3 inches of water. Bring the water to a boil. It is difficult to tenderize yuca, so it will take about 40 minutes. Drain. Cut into manageable chunks, if necessary.

Plate and top with mojo sauce.

Pureed Yuca with Goat Cheese and Shaved Garlic

This is one of my new favorite dishes. It works great as a mashed potato substitute or as a serving base, such as polenta or grits. Try it served under the Barbecued Shrimp Skewers (pg 45) or under slices of the Skirt Steak with Chimichuri (pg 70).

Ingredients

2 pounds of frozen yuca

1 tablespoon of salt

¾ cup of goats milk or Half and Half

4 ounces of goat cheese

2 tablespoons of olive oil

4 cloves of garlic, shaved or thinly sliced

Preparation

Cover the frozen yucca pieces with 2-3 inches of water. Bring the water to a boil. It is difficult to tenderize yuca, so boil for 1 hour or until fork tender. Drain.

Puree the yuca in a food processor, adding the milk and goat cheese incrementally as it begins to loosen. You can choose how dry or wet you prefer your yuca by adding the cream in small amounts.

Slice or shave the garlic. (I prefer to shave it with a small mandolin made specifically for garlic.) Lightly sweat the garlic in the olive oil over low heat.

Before serving stir in the garlic oil mixture.

Yuca Frita with Curry Dipping Sauce

This is a great side dish to go along with just about anything. It can also be used as an appetizer or a snack. While it sounds exotic, I have found that kids and people with a less adventurous palate also love these.

The initial phase of this recipe is very similar to how you prepare the boiled yuca. It is important to note that the boiling time is significantly shorter in this recipe. Do not confuse the two.

Ingredients

1 pound of frozen yuca

2 quarts of vegetable oil

1 tablespoon of salt

Curry Dipping Sauce (pg 103)

Preparation

Cover the frozen yuca pieces with 2-3 inches of water. Bring the water to a boil. It is difficult to tenderize yuca, so it will take about 30 minutes to sufficiently soften them. They become tender when the fibers appear to almost fray. Slice into strips about 3 inches long and rough ½ inch thick, removing the heavier cord like pieces in the center.

Drain and gently pat the strips dry. In a large deep pan or fryer, heat the oil to 350 degrees. Fry the yuca for 3-4 minutes, keeping the heat at 350 degrees and the yuca moving. When done, shake away the excess oil.

Serve with Curry Dipping Sauce (pg 103).

Desserts & Sweets

How you finish a good meal is as important as how you start one. Or so my wife has told me repeatedly. All joking aside, I do love the idea of a beautiful dessert. Desserts are their own art form, the balancing of rich, sweet flavors and the need to not overpower the meal can be a complex task. I think the handful of recipes I have included in this section do a good job of finding that balance. Enjoy.

Pineapple Flambé with Vanilla Bean Ice Cream

Everyone thinks of Bananas Foster or Banana Flambé, but more often than not people don't realize just how good pineapple can be when done in this manner. This is so easy and so elegant that it is as much a show as a dessert.

It really doesn't matter which rum you use as long as the proof is high enough to flame. You can make your own ice cream, but any good quality ice cream works.

Ingredients

1 medium sized, ripe pineapple

½ cup raw or brown sugar

½ stick of unsalted butter (about ¼ cup)

3 ounces of dark rum

1 quart of vanilla bean ice cream

Preparation

Peel and core the pineapple. Slice it into rings about ¾ thick. Pat dry and coat evenly in sugar. In a small sauce pan warm the rum, but DO NOT bring to a boil. In a large heavy skillet, melt butter and heat to medium level. Brown the slices of pineapple until golden. About 3 minutes per side.

Remove the skillet from heat and add the warmed rum. Ignite the rum. Then return the skillet to stovetop and burn off excess alcohol. Let it rest for a few minutes to allow the sauce to slightly thicken, but not reach room temperature. Serve each ring with a single scoop of the ice cream and a few spoonfuls of the sauce.

Banana Chocolate Papusas

My wife complained that there was a distinct lack of chocolate in my desserts. I had to agree with her. So I went into the kitchen and played with some ideas for a chocolate dessert. What I came up with was a very unorthodox version of a papusa.

I've sweetened the masa harina and filled it with bananas and chocolate, then dusted the entire fried goodness with cocoa powder and powdered sugar.

Ingredients

2 cups of masa harina

1 cup of water

2 tablespoons of sugar

3 ripe bananas

¼ cup of milk chocolate chips

¼ cup of cocoa powder

¼ cup of powdered sugar

Preparation

Sift the sugar and masa harina until evenly blended. Gradually add the 1 cup of warm water to the masa harina and mix by hand. Form 2- 2 inch ball of dough. Flatten each ball by using a tortilla press or by placing between two sheets of parchment paper and flattening.

Cut the bananas into thin slices. Layer about 10 sliced into the center of one of the flattened rounds. Add about 10 chocolate chips. Place the other round on top of the filling. Crimp the edges of the papusa. Place oil in a shallow frying pan and heat. Fry each papusa for three minutes on each side, or until starting to brown

Dust with the cocoa and powdered sugar.

Pumpkin Apple Tres Leches

     The traditional cake is a white sponge or butter cake, soaked in three types of milk (tres leches) and topped with whipped cream. My first taste of this cake was in a coffee shop in Panama. This variation substitutes a pumpkin spice cake.

Ingredients

2 cups of pumpkin puree

2 cups of flour

3 large eggs

1 ½ cups of sugar

½ cup of apple sauce

2 teaspoons of baking soda

½ teaspoon of salt

1 teaspoon of cinnamon

1 teaspoon of powdered ginger

½ teaspoon of ground nutmeg

⅛ teaspoon allspice

¾ cup of evaporated milk

½ cup of heavy cream

¾ cup of sweetened condensed milk

Whipped cream

(continued on next page)

Pumpkin Apple Tres Leches (cont.)

Preparation

In a medium size bowl combine flour, baking soda, spices and salt. In a mixing bowl combine pumpkin, applesauce and sugar. Add in eggs and thoroughly mix. Combine the contents of the two bowls and beat until mixed evenly.

Pour batter into a greased 9x13 baking dish. Place in an oven preheated to 350 degrees and bake for 30 minutes or until it tests done with a toothpick. Using a fork or toothpick place holes in the cake.

Combine the condensed milk, the evaporated milk and the heavy cream. Pour over the cake and chill.

Serve in squares with whipped cream.

Mango-Peach Dessert Soup

Dessert soups sound odd at first. But they provide a nice dessert on hot tropical nights. The creaminess and fruit sweetness provide a nice finish. I have encountered a wide variety of fruits used in dessert soups, but I prefer the mango and peach combination.

Ingredients

1 cup of mango nectar

½ cup of sweetened condensed milk

2 ripe peaches

2 ripe mangos

1 tablespoon of sugar

1 small container of Greek yogurt

Preparation

Peel and pit the mangos and peaches. In a blender, puree the fruit with the sugar. While blending, pour in the sweetened condensed milk and mango nectar. Chill and serve in small bowls or sundae dishes. Top with a small dollop of yogurt. This adds a decorative touch but also cuts the sweetness.

Limber de Coco (Puerto Rican Coconut Ice Pops)

These coconut ice pops are a Puerto Rican treasure. My wife, Christa, is so fond of these that she insisted I include them in the desserts. The traditional way of eating Limber de Coco, is similar to the push up pops many of us ate growing up. In order to do this, you need to freeze the ingredients in either small paper or plastic cups. You can, however, freeze them in ramekins for a more sophisticated presentation.

Ingredients

1-15 ounce can of sweet coconut cream

1-13 ounce can of coconut milk

1 cup of half and half

1 cup of water

¼ cup of sweetened shredded coconut

1 teaspoon of vanilla extract

1 teaspoon of cinnamon

Preparation

It really doesn't get much easier than this. Place all of the ingredients into a blender and mix. Pour the mixture into the containers of your choice. Cover the tops with plastic wrap, leaving space between the liquid and the wrap. Place the containers in the freezer for 24 hours.

Tropical Fruit Salad

Who doesn't enjoy a cool fruit salad on a hot day? How could you improve on it? Easy — use tropical fruit and a special syrup. Here's how.

Ingredients

1 small pineapple

1 quart of strawberries

¼ cup of sweetened coconut flakes

1 large ripe mango

2 cups of orange juice

1 cup of sugar

10-12 mint leaves

Preparation

Peel, core and dice the pineapple. Clean and quarter the strawberries. Peel, pit and dice the mango. Place all the fruit in a large non-reactive bowl.

Place the orange juice, sugar and mint leaves in a sauce pan. Reduce by ½. Let cool. Remove the mint leaves. Pour over the fruit mixture. Sprinkle in the sweetened coconut flakes.

Sauces & Marinades

Sauces are an important part of any culinary experience. They can be the foundations of some complex dishes or they can be accents added to give flair to a relatively simple piece of grilled meat or fish.

Marinades are the building blocks of flavor in so many dishes. It's always good to have a few at your disposal.

This section will provide you with a variety of sauces and marinades that can play multiple roles in your meals. Many of these are important components in creating some of other recipes.

Balsamic Reduction

A simple balsamic reduction has a ton of uses and is not complicated. While it can be time consuming to prepare, it is worth it. The reduction is used in several recipes in this book such as Stuffed Sweet Peppers with Balsamic Reduction (pg 33) and Whole Grilled Plantain (pg 83). In addition to the recipes found here, it is a rich, bold addition to many other foods.

Ingredients

1 cup of Balsamic Vinegar

¼ cup of honey

Preparation

In a sauce pan mix the honey and vinegar. Bring to a boil. Reduce the heat and simmer until the volume is reduced by approximately 2/3. This should take about 15 to 20 minutes.

Chimichurri

This simple but elegant sauce comes from the Argentine tradition of serving great grilled meats. There isn't a steakhouse in Latin America that doesn't have some version of the sauce setting on the table. My personal favorites come from an Argentine steakhouse in Panama and a huge outdoor grill in Guatemala. This is my take on combining the two variations.

It can also double as a marinade for just about any red meat. Make a batch and keep it on hand. It will keep in a refrigerator for about a week if you store it in an air tight container. After refrigeration, let it return to room temperature and whisk.

Ingredients

¼ cup of finely chopped flat leaf parsley

2 tablespoons of finely chopped oregano leaf

2 teaspoons of garlic, finely chopped

2 teaspoons of crushed red pepper flakes

½ teaspoon of salt

Juice of 1 medium sized lemon

3 tablespoons of red wine vinegar

½ cup of extra-virgin olive oil

Preparation

Mix the dry ingredients in a non-reactive bowl. Add red wine vinegar and lemon juice. Gently muddle. Add extra-virgin olive oil. Whisk. Let stand for at least two hours for the flavors to mix. Whisk and serve.

Curry Dipping Sauce

I have had several wonderful variations of this sauce in locations as varied as Trinidad, Costa Rica and St. Louis, Missouri. When I first attempted to replicate the variations I had eaten, I seemed to always make it more complicated than it needed to be. This is the one my family and friends seem to enjoy the most, it is also one of the simplest but most flavorful recipes in the book.

This dipping sauce pairs nicely with the Yucca Frita (pg 89) and the Tostones (pg 81). I have also served it with chopped raw vegetables and even simple grilled chicken kebabs.

Ingredients

1 tablespoon of yellow curry powder

1 teaspoon of sea salt

¼ teaspoon of sugar

½ teaspoon of lemon juice

4 ounces of plain Greek yogurt

Preparations

Combine curry powder, salt and sugar in a small bowl. Add lemon juice. Add yogurt a little at a time while whipping it until it has a smooth texture.

Ginger-Honey Soy Sauce

This was created as a sauce for seared tuna steaks, but it works well as marinade for just about anything you are going to grill. It is ridiculously simple, but adds a great flavor. It can be stored in an airtight container for several days.

Ingredients

1 cup of soy sauce (you can use low sodium, but it has a less strong flavor when marinating)

1 ounce of puréed ginger

2 tablespoons of honey

1 teaspoon of sesame oil

Preparation

In a small sauce pan warm the soy sauce, add the honey and dissolve completely, add the ginger puree. Remove from heat and allow to cool. Add the sesame oil, which will allow it to coat whatever you plan on marinating.

Guava Chipotle Barbecue Sauce

Since the very first time I tried guava, I loved it. It has sweetness and an inherent, almost smoky after taste. It seemed to be a natural for adding to a barbecue sauce. Being a fan of a little bit of heat in my barbecue, I knew I needed a pepper added to the mix. It turned out that guava and chipotle complement each other.

This sauce is used in the recipes for Barbecued Pork Medallions (pg 55) and Barbecue Shrimp Skewers (pg 45).

The sauce can be stored in the refrigerator for up to a week. It can also be frozen.

Ingredients

2 cups of guava nectar

1 cup of ketchup

1 tablespoon of garlic, chopped

11 ounce can of chipotle peppers in adobo

4 ounces of guava paste

Preparation

Pour 2 cups of room temperature guava nectar in a sauce pan. I prefer the nectar sold in cardboard or glass containers to those in aluminum, but any can be used. Add chopped garlic and guava paste. Begin to heat slowly. The guava paste will begin to soften and melt. Add the peppers. As it heats, add the ketchup. Bring to a low boil and let simmer for 10 minutes.

Let the mixture cool and pour into a blender. Blend until smooth.

Jerk Marinade

If you want aromatic, sweet and hot, then you want Jamaican Jerk. This is a great marinade for poultry, meat or fish. It blends all of the island spices to come up with a unique flavor that isn't for the faint of heart. It takes time to make and the marinating time varies from dish to dish, but any hassle is definitely worth it.

It is used in the Jerk Chicken Kebabs (pg 56) and Jerk Pork Chops (pg 59)

Ingredients

2 habanero peppers

½ cup of chopped green onion

8 cloves of garlic

1 tablespoon of herbes de provence

1 tablespoon of all spice

1 teaspoon of nutmeg

½ tablespoon of cinnamon

¼ cup of brown sugar

½ cup of soy sauce

1/3 cup of lime juice

2 tablespoons of vegetable oil

Preparation

Stem and seed the habanero peppers. Place all ingredients into a food processor and blend until smooth. It can be stored for up to 1 week before use.

Mojo

This is a great marinade and sauce for grilled chicken, fish or pork. If you use a fish, a firm white fish or a whole fish is recommended.

There are literally countless versions of mojo. Every grandmother has her own version and everybody thinks their grandma's is the perfect version. This is, of course, a matter of personal taste and opinion. That being said, this my version, obviously the best version, although I'm a middle aged man and not a grandmother.

Ingredients

1 cup of orange juice

½ cup of lime juice

½ cup of lemon juice

¼ cup of coarsely chopped oregano

¼ cup of olive oil

3 tablespoons of garlic, chopped

2 habanero peppers

1 teaspoon of salt

1 teaspoon of sugar

Preparation

Clean and seed the peppers. In a non-reactive bowl add all ingredients. Stir until salt is dissolved and the spices appear evenly distributed. The finished mojo can be refrigerated for up to one week.

Red Pepper and Tomato Dipping Sauce

While this may not sound like a beach dish, a friend of mine who grew up on the East Coast of the United States described a similar sauce from his boardwalk days. It was served with fried clams, as well as, boiled and fried shrimp. In my experience, it works well with fried calamari or just about anything fried.

Ingredients

2-6 ounce cans of quality tomato paste

2 tablespoons of balsamic vinegar

2 tablespoons of dry vermouth

2 tablespoons of chopped oregano

1 tablespoon of garlic, chopped

2 teaspoons of crushed red pepper flakes

1 teaspoon of brown sugar

Preparations

In a sauce pan add tomato paste, vermouth and vinegar. Heat until the paste loosens, then add garlic, sugar and red pepper. Let it simmer for 2-3 minutes. Add oregano and simmer for 2 more minutes.

Measurement Conversions

Volume Conversions	
Imperial	**Metric**
1 teaspoon	5 mL
1 tablespoon or 1/2 fluid ounce	15 mL
1 fluid ounce or 1/8 cup	30 mL
1/4 cup or 2 fluid ounces	60 mL
1/3 cup	80 mL
1/2 cup or 4 fluid ounces	120 mL
2/3 cup	160 mL
3/4 cup or 6 fluid ounces	180 mL
1 cup or 8 fluid ounces or half a pint	240 mL
1 1/2 cups or 12 fluid ounces	350 mL
2 cups or 1 pint or 16 fluid ounces	475 mL
3 cups or 1 1/2 pints	700 mL
4 cups or 2 pints or 1 quart	950 mL
4 quarts or 1 gallon	3.8 L

Weight Conversions	
Imperial	**Metric**
1 ounce	28 g
4 ounces or 1/4 pound	113 g
1/3 pound	150 g
8 ounces or 1/2 pound	230 g
2/3 pound	300 g
12 ounces or 3/4 pound	340 g
1 pound or 16 ounces	450 g
2 pounds	900 g

Index

Subscribe to my blog and receive a free recipe for my richly delicious Mango Cannoli
www.beachblanketbistro.com